599.6475
S

Mountain Goats

by Lindsay Shaffer

BELLWETHER MEDIA • MINNEAPOLIS, MN

BLASTOFF!
2
READERS

Note to Librarians, Teachers, and Parents:

Blastoff! Readers are carefully developed by literacy experts and combine standards-based content with developmentally appropriate text.

Level 1 provides the most support through repetition of high-frequency words, light text, predictable sentence patterns, and strong visual support.

Level 2 offers early readers a bit more challenge through varied simple sentences, increased text load, and less repetition of high-frequency words.

Level 3 advances early-fluent readers toward fluency through increased text and concept load, less reliance on visuals, longer sentences, and more literary language.

Level 4 builds reading stamina by providing more text per page, increased use of punctuation, greater variation in sentence patterns, and increasingly challenging vocabulary.

Level 5 encourages children to move from "learning to read" to "reading to learn" by providing even more text, varied writing styles, and less familiar topics.

Whichever book is right for your reader, Blastoff! Readers are the perfect books to build confidence and encourage a love of reading that will last a lifetime!

This edition first published in 2020 by Bellwether Media, Inc.

No part of this publication may be reproduced in whole or in part without written permission of the publisher. For information regarding permission, write to Bellwether Media, Inc., Attention: Permissions Department, 6012 Blue Circle Drive, Minnetonka, MN 55343.

Library of Congress Cataloging-in-Publication Data

Names: Shaffer, Lindsay, author.
Title: Mountain Goats / by Lindsay Shaffer.
Description: Minneapolis, MN : Bellwether Media, Inc., [2020] |
   Series: Blastoff! Readers: Animals of the Mountains | Includes bibliographical references and index. |
   Audience: Age 5-8. | Audience: K to Grade 3.
Identifiers: LCCN 2018061020 (print) | LCCN 2019001616 (ebook) | ISBN 9781618915559 (ebook) |
   ISBN 9781644870143 (hardcover : alk. paper)
Subjects: LCSH: Mountain goat--Juvenile literature.
Classification: LCC QL737.U53 (ebook) | LCC QL737.U53 S46 2020 (print) | DDC 599.64/75--dc23
LC record available at https://lccn.loc.gov/2018061020

Editor: Kate Moening
Printed in the United States o

Table of Contents

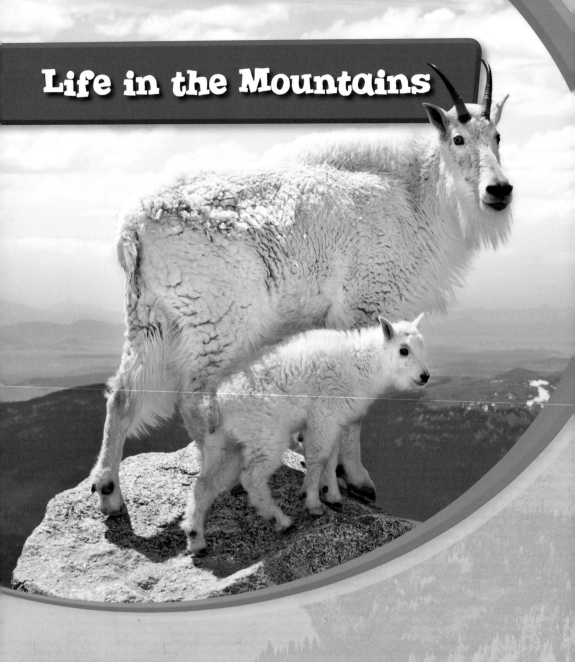

Life in the Mountains

Mountain goats are
master mountain climbers!

These **mammals** live in the mountains of western Canada and the United States.

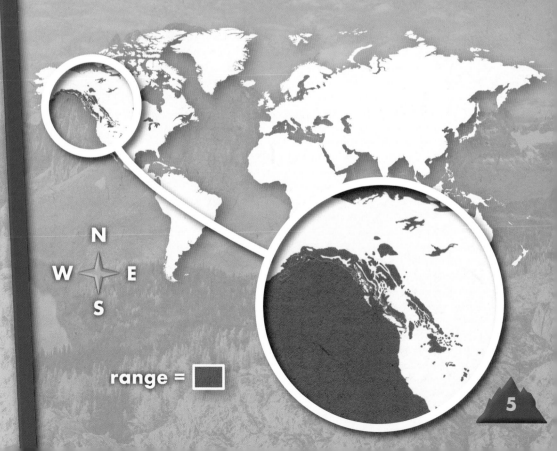

Mountain Goat Range

N
W E
S

range = ☐

Mountain goats have **adapted** to live at high **elevations**. Some have been found higher than 13,000 feet (4,000 meters)!

These climbers love their cold mountain **biome**!

Mountain goats stay warm in the cold! Their woolly **coats** grow two layers during winter.

guard hairs

white, woolly coats

cloven hooves

rubbery hoof pads

The inner layer is thick and soft. Outer **guard hairs** help mountain goats stay dry.

9

White coats **camouflage** mountain goats. The goats easily hide from **predators**.

They almost disappear
on snowy mountain slopes!

Climbing High

Mountain goats have **cloven hooves** made for climbing. Their hooves allow them to grab rocks.

Rubbery hoof pads
give them **traction**.

cloven hoof

Mountain goats are strong.
They pull themselves up
steep slopes. Predators
struggle to follow!

Mountain Goat Stats

Least Concern	Near Threatened	Vulnerable	Endangered	Critically Endangered	Extinct in the Wild	Extinct

conservation status: least concern

life span: about 12 years

If they are cornered, mountain goats fight! Strong horns help keep them safe.

A Mountain Menu

Mountain goats **forage** for many different plants. Grasses are favorite foods.

Mountain goats are not picky. They also eat pine needles, ferns, and mosses!

foraging

In early summer, mountain goats search for special **minerals**.

licking minerals

Mountain Goat Diet

bluegrass

feather moss

ponderosa pine

They travel to cliffsides
rich in these minerals.
Then they lick the rocks!

Thick winter snows bury mountain plants. Some mountain goats must travel to lower elevations to find food.

These amazing climbers run up and down mountains with ease!

21

Glossary

adapted—changed over a long period of time

biome—a large area with certain plants, animals, and weather

camouflage—to use colors and patterns to help an animal hide in its surroundings

cloven hooves—hard foot coverings that are split into two toes

coats—the hair or fur covering some animals

elevations—the heights of places

forage—to search for food

guard hairs—long, thick hairs on the outside of a mountain goat's coat

mammals—warm-blooded animals that have backbones and feed their young milk

minerals—elements found in the earth that are needed to stay healthy

predators—animals that hunt other animals for food

traction—the ability to avoid slipping on a surface while moving

To Learn More

AT THE LIBRARY

Borgert-Spaniol, Megan. *Mountain Goats*. Minneapolis, Minn.: Bellwether Media, 2018.

Davies, Monika. *How High Up the Mountain?: Mountain Animal Habitats*. Mankato, Minn.: Amicus Illustrated, 2019.

Riggs, Kate. *Antelopes*. Mankato, Minn.: Creative Education/Creative Paperbacks, 2016.

ON THE WEB

FACTSURFER

Factsurfer.com gives you a safe, fun way to find more information.

1. Go to www.factsurfer.com.

2. Enter "mountain goats" into the search box and click 🔍.

3. Select your book cover to see a list of related web sites.

Index

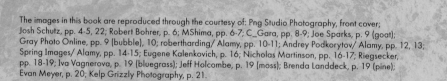

The images in this book are reproduced through the courtesy of: Png Studio Photography, front cover; Josh Schutz, pp. 4-5, 22; Robert Bohrer, p. 6; MShima, pp. 6-7; C_Gara, pp. 8-9; Joe Sparks, p. 9 (goat); Gray Photo Online, p. 9 (bubble), 10; robertharding/ Alamy, pp. 10-11; Andrey Podkorytov/ Alamy, pp. 12, 13; Spring Images/ Alamy, pp. 14-15; Eugene Kalenkovich, p. 16; Nicholas Martinson, pp. 16-17; Riegsecker, pp. 18-19; Iva Vagnerova, p. 19 (bluegrass); Jeff Holcombe, p. 19 (moss); Brenda Landdeck, p. 19 (pine); Evan Meyer, p. 20; Kelp Grizzly Photography, p. 21.